spot

CREEPY CRAWLIES

WALKING STICKS

by Nessa Black

AMICUS | AMICUS INK

body

mouth

Look for these words and pictures as you read.

eye

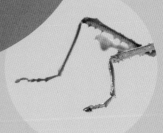

legs

Is that a twig? No.

It is a bug!

It is called a walking stick.

Look at its body.
It looks like a stick.
It can hide in a tree.

body

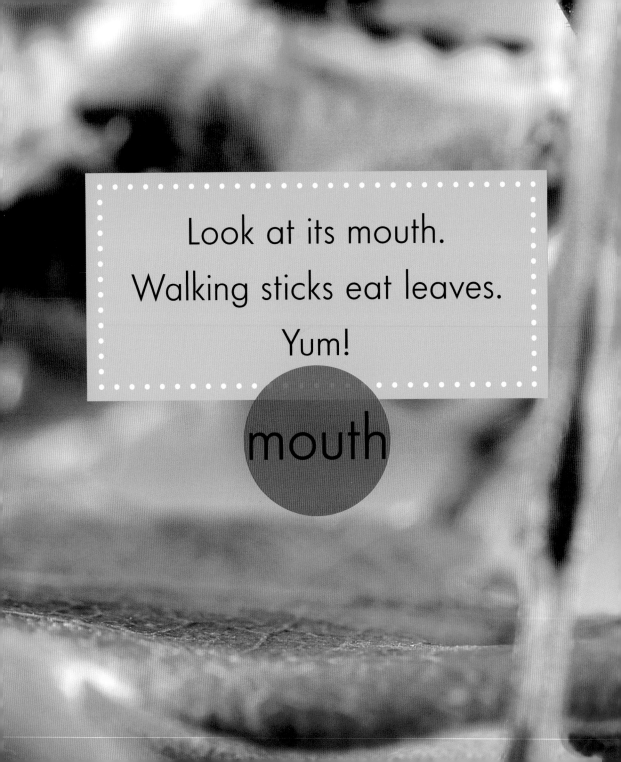

Look at its mouth.
Walking sticks eat leaves.
Yum!

mouth

It is daytime.
The walking stick stays still.
It moves around at night.

eye

Look at its eye.
The walking stick can see well.
It sees best in dim light.

Look at its legs.
A bird comes near.
The bug waves its legs.
The bird stays back.

legs

These bugs know
how to stay safe!

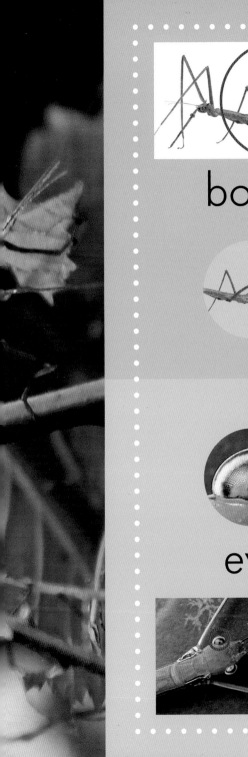

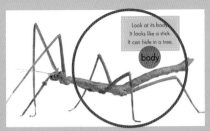

Look at its body.
It looks like a stick.
It can hide in a tree.

body

body

Look at its mouth.
Walking sticks eat leaves.
Yum!

mouth

mouth

Did you find?

eye

Look at its eye.
The walking stick can see well.
It sees best in dim light.

eye

legs

Look at its legs.
A bird comes near.
The bug waves its legs.
The bird stays back.

legs

Spot is published by Amicus and Amicus Ink
P.O. Box 1329, Mankato, MN 56002
www.amicuspublishing.us

Library of Congress Cataloging-in-Publication Data
Names: Black, Nessa, author.
Title: Walking sticks / by Nessa Black.
Description: Mankato, MN : Amicus/Amicus Ink, [2019] |
   Series: Spot. Creepy crawlies | Audience: K to grade 3.
Identifiers: LCCN 2017046901 (print) | LCCN 2017050588
   (ebook) | ISBN 9781681515786 (pdf) | ISBN
   9781681515403 (library binding) | ISBN 9781681523781
   (pbk.)
Subjects: LCSH: Stick insects–Juvenile literature.
Classification: LCC QL509.5 (ebook) | LCC QL509.5 .B53
   2019 (print) | DDC 595.7/29–dc23
LC record available at https://lccn.loc.gov/2017046901

Printed in China

HC   10 9 8 7 6 5 4 3 2 1
PB   10 9 8 7 6 5 4 3 2 1

Wendy Dieker and Alissa Thielges,
   editors
Deb Miner, series designer
Kazuko Collins, book designer
Holly Young, photo researcher

Photos by iStock/NNehring cover;
Shutterstock/Andrew Burgess 1, Jack
Hong 3, Eric Isselee 4–5, itsmejust 6–7,
reisegraf.ch 8–9, SIMON SHIM 10–11,
Zoltan Major 14; Storyblocks 12–13

WALKING STICKS